Bridges:
To There

Poems for Mind, Body
& Spirit

Gary W. Burns

WWW.TURNINGCORNERBOOKS.COM

Copyright © 2014 by Vista View Publishing

Published by:
Turning Corner Books
PO Box 121
Haymarket, VA 20168

All rights reserved under International
And Pan-American Copyright Conventions.

Library of Congress Control Number: 2010930366
ISBN: 978-0-9827805-6-5

Fourth Printing, February 2018

Designed by the author; artwork by the author unless otherwise noted.

- Front Cover and Title Page: Water Lilies and Japanese Bridge, Claude Monet; Princeton University Art Museum: faithful photographic reproduction, public domain; Wikimedia Commons
- Back Cover: Spring Night, Harlem River, Ernest Lawson; The Phillips Collection: faithful photographic reproduction, public domain; Wikimedia Commons
- Page 15: Ulrung-Do, South Korea: by Author
- Page 25: Palace Grounds, Tokyo, Japan: by Author
- Page 33: Golden Gate Bridge, San Francisco, California, USA , public domain
- Pages 45, 49, 85 & 91: Kyoto, Japan: by Author
- Page 57: Pont Genois de Pianella, Ota, Corse-du-Sud, France: by Myrabella, Wikimedia Commons, public domain
  (This picture may be reproduced; see Wikimedia Commons for criteria)
- Page 65: Cherry Blossom Festival: Chinhae, South Korea: by Author
- Page 77: Cape Cod Canal, Massachusetts, USA: USACE
- Page 99: Pohang, South Korea: by Mia Burns

No part of this book may be reproduced in any form without permission in writing from the publisher; except by a reviewer, who may quote brief passages in a review to be printed in a magazine, newspaper or posted to the World Wide Web. Particular emphasis is laid on the matter of broadcasting, recording and public performance.

Aerial

Suspension

Crossing

Banks

Other Books of Poetry by Gary W. Burns

Clouds: On the Wind
(Poems for the Soul – A Meditation)

Earth Tones: A Journey
(Poetry for the Journey)

Garden Walks: Hand In Hand
(Poems To Relax By)

Moments: This to the Next
(Poetry - Now and Eternity)

Poems of Love: A Selection Vol. I

Poems of Love: A Selection Vol. II

Rainy Day: Wondering
(Poems for a Rainy Day)

Twilight: Awaking the Stars
(Poems of the Night's Light)

To Pam
For Her Artistic Spirit

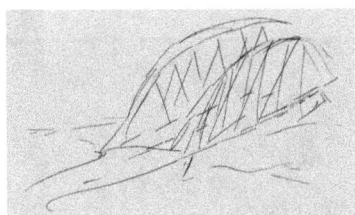

Contents

Aerial

You	17
The Work Of Art	18
The Wind All About	19
Every Hue	20
Love	21
Of True	22
Being Grateful	23
Freedoms Compliment	24
Tao	26
Freely	27
Old Astrologers Delight	28
The Perfect Light	29
Illusions Wall	30
Flow	31

Suspension

The Spirit of Love	35
Love Tells Me	36
Compassion	37
Unlimited	38
The Fire	39
Cosmic	40
Meditative Nuance	41
Eternity Lovingly	42
Truly	43
Harmonious	44
Hold Dear	46
Halfway	47
Insightful	48
Time and Harmony	50
Tranquility In Bridges: To There	51
Ramblers Care	52
Be of Good Cheer	53
Cooing of the Dove	54
Calling	55

Crossing

Perhaps	59
Reflection	60
Aware	61
Your Dear Friend	62
Differences	63
Balance	
In Bridges: To There	64
Intimacy	66
Quiescence	67
All Cloudy	68
Windows Away	69
Your Longing	70
Us	71
Harmony's Way	72
Joining	73
Surely	74
Body Corporal	75

Banks

A Rhythm A Rhyme	79
Dearest	80
Natures Care	81
Treasure	82
Ubiquitous	83
Contemplation	84
Journey's Mystery	86
Dialogue	87
Bridges	88
Potential's Way	89
Zen Garden	90
Spiritual Boon	92
Take Heart	93
Deep, Close	94
Crossed	95
Way	96
Brush Strokes	97
Traveler	98
Imagination's Door	99

Aerial

Bridges: To There

You

Whatever you do

Don't hesitate
To celebrate

You

Bridges: To There

The Work Of Art

*Clouds
Are breaking
The blue
Of the sky*

*Pieces of blue
Are everywhere,*

*But,
Nothing's falling apart:
Painting
The work of art.*

Bridges: To There

The Wind All About

In the trees, with ease
The bird flees the stir of leaves

When the spirit of the wind
Stirs us
Go we must

Bridges: To There

Every Hue

*Think of the sky
In shades of blue*

*Life
Every hue*

Bridges: To There

Love

Yesterday
They spoke of you
And today
They do too

Rain drops
Nurturing

Love

Bridges: To There

Of True

*In the universe
Of true*

*There's me
And
There's you*

Bridges: To There

Being Grateful

Being grateful

The great dance
Took place

Grace

Bridges: To There

Freedoms Compliment

*Holding
    because I love you*

*Letting go
    because again I do*

Love you

Bridges: To There

Tao

*Don't change
Now
Into moments,
Or hours,
Or days
Or
Into a lifetime*

*Be
Here
Be
Now*

*Blissful
Tao*

Bridges: To There

Freely

Free,
Speaking to me,
Stating openly,

"I will take you there

If
You come with me

    Freely"

Bridges: To There

Old Astrologers Delight

*To the Old Astrologers
Delight
The infinity
Of the starry night
Welcomed
Owls and stars
And stargazers alike.*

*Charting
The eyes reflection,
Configuring direction
And offering introspection
The Old Astrologers
Delight
Awoke the night.*

Bridges: To There

The Perfect Light

*Love
Is
The Perfect Light*

*Through dark night
And daylight
Alike*

Bridges: To There

Illusions Wall

Summer sun
Winter wind

Upon
Our skin

Thin

The life some call all

Bridges: To There

Flow

*Spirited
Rivers run
From the depths of the mind
To the Ocean of Life*

Suspension

Bridges: To There

The Spirit Of Love

Dear One,

Love
And I will care
*   for you.*

Yours always,
Love

Bridges: To There

Love
Tells Me

*Love
Tells me*

*Closeness
Is ecstasy*

Let's be

Bridges: To There

Compassion

*Compassion
Is living*

By giving:

*Share
In the time there is to care*

Bridges: To There

Unlimited

*The mind's eye
Sees an unlimited sky*

*Go there
And declare*

You

The Fire

The glint of the flame,
Goes off
Delicately

To where
Only imagination
Can see

Bridges: To There

Cosmic

Down corridors of solitude
Over thresholds of meditation
To the point of pointless

Cosmic

Bridges: To There

Meditative Nuance

Brown, green, ebony
Blue
With eyes anew

Look pass sadness
To gladness

Eternity Lovingly

*Filling you
Filling me*

*Eternity's
Touch*

*Love
Is that much*

Bridges: To There

Truly

Be

See
Eternity

Bridges: To There

Harmonious

Simplicity
In orders of magnitude

Bridges: To There

Hold Dear

*Quiet
Pervades the serenity
Of winter's atmosphere*

*In calm
Enjoy
The peacefulness
That winter days hold dear*

Half Way

*Meeting Spirit
Half
Way*

*Life
Is full.*

Bridges: To There

Insightfully

Crossed insightfully
Bridges take you, likely
Where you want to be

Bridges: To There

*Time
and
Harmony*

*The resonance
In the appeal to more
In the realization of less*

Bridges: To There

Tranquility

Tranquility;
The universe,
Harmony
And me.

In Bridges: To There

Bridges: To There

Ramblers Care

Knowing direction
Via introspection

Rambling brooks
Take a ramblers care
To where "there"
May take them.

Bridges: To There

Be of Good Cheer

Snowflakes lie
Upon the petals of the rose

Cold comes quickly

Be of good cheer

Bridges: To There

Cooing Of the Dove

*Here and there
Below and above*

*Offers of Love
The cooing of the Dove*

Bridges: To There

Calling

*It wasn't me
Who called*

*"Spirit
It's you I want to see"*

*It was Spirit
That called to me
Saying*

*"Spirit
You Be"*

Crossing

Perhaps

Perhaps
To get to there
You needn't go far

"There"
May be where you are

Reflection

Reflection;
We
Viewing eternity

Bridges: To There

Aware

Aware

Of the union
Of universe and heart

Care
For every part

Bridges: To There

Your Dear Friend

For end
There's begin

For begin
There's end

That's why
Now
Is your dear friend

Bridges: To There

Differences

*Be
As the blue of the sky*

*Not contemplating
Differences
Or caring why*

Balance

Feel the going
Know the on

In Bridges: To There

Bridges: To There

Intimacy

Breath
We are the wind

Quench
We are the sea

O the intimacy

Bridges: To There

Quiescence

Quiet
Alone

Deep breath
Peaceful

Calm
Encompassing

All Cloudy

Clouds
In their amorphous wonder

Clouds
In their mistiness

Clouds
In their flowing

Clouds
In their coming and going

We
All cloudy

Bridges: To There

Windows Away

*We are only
Windows away*

*I see you there
You see me here*

*Our togetherness
Is clear*

Bridges: To There

Your Longing

The singing of songs
You choose to sing
Will bring

Your longing

Us

*A purpose
To fulfill*

Bridges: To There

Harmony's Way

*Today
Into tomorrow
And tomorrow
Into another today;
Harmony's
Way*

Bridges: To There

Joining

I've walked away,
But,
Never from a friend
Or a lover

Only from myself

To join you

To celebrate
Us

Bridges: To There

Surely

Surely
What you see in me
Are thoughts of you

It's the mirror
That's true

Bridges: To There

Body Corporal

*The flock
Making wing*

*Is
Guided*

By the stars

Banks

Bridges: To There

A Rhythm A Rhyme

Tears
Emptiness
Fears

Echoes
In the mind
Seeking to find
A rhythm a rhyme

Honor
The banquet host
The most

And you'll find
A rhythm
A rhyme

Dearest

The winter wren
Low to the ground
Close to the sound

Of the Earth
Going round, round, round

Knows
Dearest
Spirit

Bridges: To There

Natures Care

Beauty

*Moving
Tree to tree
And within
The green scenery
Reaches
You and me*

*Offering
The pleasantry*

*Of peacefulness,
Bliss
And happiness.*

*Dare
To venture to there,
Share
Natures care.*

Treasure

*Take time to cherish
And understand*

> *The love
>   At hand*

Bridges: To There

Ubiquitous

Time exhales
Our final breath

Bridges: To There

Contemplation

Words

*Make up your mind
To leave them behind
Find*

Bliss

Bridges: To There

Journey's Mystery

Each turn
In every road
Leads,

We follow

Journey's
Mystery

Dialogue

The forsythia and daffodil
Corresponding

Bring
Spring

Bridges: To There

Bridges

Bridges;

*The winds
Hidden from sight,
The sun
Burning bright,
The stars
Twinkling through night*

*The calm and frothy seas,
The seasonal breeze*

*The mother, the father,
The child
The sister, the brother,
The lover*

The friend

*Me
And you too*

Bridges: To There

Potential's Way

1
*Prints
In icy snow;
Steps taken
A time ago.*

2
*It's a stifling whim
To live within
Was
Or could have been.*

3
*Leave behind
Thoughts that blind
Heart and mind.*

4
*Rejoice
In today, live
Potential's
        Way.*

Bridges: To There

Zen Garden

The heartbeats' symphony
Sounds life
In harmony
With eternity

Bridges: To There

Bridges: To There

Spiritual Boon

The glow of the snow
Under the light of the moon

The warm spring
That's gone all to soon

The dance of summer
With flowers in bloom

The colorful leaves that fall
To autumns call

Spiritual boon
All

Bridges: To There

Take Heart

*It's
Not so much
The door*

As it is

*The
Way*

Deep, Close

Viewing the stars
One winter's night
High
From an alpine height

Clothed
In immortal dark
Bathed
In eternal light

The starry host
Gives its most

Deep, close

Bridges: To There

Crossed

To live in a world of proximate

Or live in one of absolute

Therein lies the bridge Dragon

Crossed
    All
    Knows
    Small

Bridges: To There

Way

Magical

*The
Way*

*Sunday
Gives way
To Monday*

Bridges: To There

Brush Strokes

Upon the master palette

Spirited

Imagination swirls

And clouds
Silver, white and gray
Make a day

Bridges: To There

Traveler

*Gentleness
Goes easy*

*Be
On your way
Traveler*

Bridges: To There

Imagination's Door

*Imagination's door
Can make life more*

ABOUT THE AUTHOR

Inspired by nature and the beauty around him Gary W. Burns started writing poetry at a young age. Early on Gary was able to express his thoughts, ideas and emotions through the vivid imagery of his verse. His poetry has been published in various literary arts journals, anthologies and magazines. He is the author of 10 books of poetry. Through his poems Gary shares his reflections on the many facets of life and on the beauty of nature. The expressiveness of his poetry has been enriched by his wide reading in philosophy and psychology. He has traveled throughout the world and has lived in numerous countries, to include, Italy, Korea, Saudi Arabia and Canada. He has also lived in Hawaii and several other states. Currently, Gary makes his home in Northern Virginia near the foothills of the Blue Ridge Mountains

ENJOY THESE OTHER BOOKS OF POETRY BY GARY W. BURNS

Clouds: On the Wind
(Poems for the Soul - A Meditation)
ISBN: 978-0-9845342-0-2 (Paperback)
ISBN: 978-0-9845342-1-0 (Hardcover)
ISBN: 978-0-9860900-3-5 (E-Book)

Twilight: Awaking the Stars
(Poems of the Night's Light)
ISBN: 978-0-9845342-7-2 (Paperback)
ISBN: 978-0-9827805-4-1 (Hardcover)
ISBN: 978-0-9860900-6-6 (E-Book)

Earth Tones: A Journey
(Poetry for the Journey)
ISBN: 978-0-9845342-6-5 (Paperback)
ISBN: 978-0-9845342-9-6 (Hardcover)
ISBN: 978-0-9860900-8-0 (E-Book)

Available at WWW.TURNINGCORNERBOOKS.COM and where books are sold.

Dawn and Beyond: Embark
(Poetry - Come Destiny)
ISBN: 978-0-9827805-8-9 (Paperback)
ISBN: 978-0-9827805-9-6 (Hardcover)
ISBN: 978-0-9860900-0-4 (E-Book)

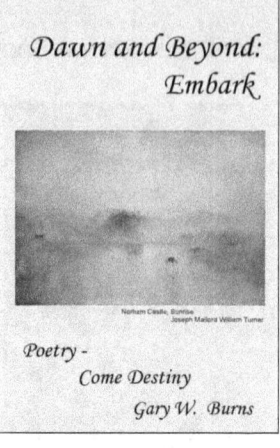

Moments: This to the Next
(Poetry - Now and Eternity)
ISBN: 978-0-9845342-4-1 (Paperback)
ISBN: 978-0-9827805-1-0 (Hardcover)
ISBN: 978-0-9860900-9-7 (E-Book)

Rainy Day: Wondering
(Poems for a Rainy Day)
ISBN: 978-0-9845342-5-8 (Paperback)
ISBN: 978-0-9827805-2-7 (Hardcover)
ISBN: 978-0-9860900-7-3 (E-Book)

Available at WWW.TURNINGCORNERBOOKS.COM and where books are sold.

Poems of Love: Selection Vol. II
ISBN: 979-8-9909248-0-2 (Paperback)
ISBN: 979-8-9909248-1-9 (Hardcover)
ISBN: 979-8-9909248-2-6 (E-Book)

Garden Walks: Hand In Hand
(Poems To Relax By)
ISBN: 978-0-9845342-3-4 (Paperback)
ISBN: 978-0-9827805-0-3 (Hardcover)
ISBN: 978-0-9860900-1-1 (E-Book)

Poems of Love: A Selection Vol. I
ISBN: 978-0-9845342-8-9 (Paperback)
ISBN: 978-0-9827805-5-8 (Hardcover)
ISBN: 978-0-9860900-5-9 (E-Book)

Available at WWW.TURNINGCORNERBOOKS.COM and where books are sold.

www.ingramcontent.com/pod-product-compliance
Lightning Source LLC
Chambersburg PA
CBHW050602300426
44112CB00013B/2036